Angels

*For Rhiannon and Pip,
my 'little angels'*

Jane Williams
Angels

Illustrations by Linda Baker Smith

LION

A Lion Book
an imprint of
Lion Hudson plc
Mayfield House, 256 Banbury Road,
Oxford OX2 7DH, England
www.lionhudson.com
ISBN-13: 978-0-7459-5222-2
ISBN-10: 0-7459-5222-4

First edition 2006
10 9 8 7 6 5 4 3 2 1

Acnowledgments
Scripture quotations are taken from the New Revised Standard
Version published by HarperCollins Publishers, copyright © 1989
by the Division of Christian Education of the National Council
of the Churches of Christ in the USA, and are used by permission.
All rights reserved.

A catalogue record for this book is available
from the British Library

Typeset in 10.5/15 ElegaGarmnd BT

Printed and bound in China

Contents

Introduction

Angels feature in all religious traditions, and people of different ages and different faiths or no faith at all have encountered them. Where stories of aliens, or even of God, may meet with disbelief, stories of angels are much more likely to be heard with respect and interest. In what we think about angels, it is as though we allow ourselves access to needs that normally we would deny or suppress. Angels give us a way of expressing our longing for beings who are more powerful than ourselves, and who care for us. They let us show our desire to know that we are not the only rational and sentient beings in the universe.

Books on angels abound. Some of the writings about angels seem frankly and naively selfish. They may have titles like *How to make your angel work for you* or *Getting the best out of your angel*. Some are more reflective, pointing out that pretty well all cultures and religions have some angel equivalent. Some writers go for pseudo-science, and speculate about the connections between angels and alien stories. But all of them are convinced that 'there are more things in heaven and earth… than are dreamt of in our philosophies', and all show the human longing for friendly and protective beings in the universe.

*Angels can be found
in most cultures and
religious faiths.*

A lot of these books on angels are written by people who believe they have encountered angels, or who have collected eyewitness accounts from others who have met with angels. Some people have been alone when they met their angel, but sometimes groups of people have shared the same experience. The overwhelming majority of these experiences show angels either protecting or consoling people, though some people have been warned by angels or themselves commissioned by an angel to carry a message to someone else. If the people who meet an angel are already believers, it seems to strengthen their faith in God. But if they are not, it seems that angels are not particular.

The major religious traditions would understand these encounters with angels, but would want to put them in a broader context. Angels play significant roles in Islam, Judaism and Christianity, where their function is directly

connected with God. Their very name actually describes what they are for, rather than what they are in themselves. 'Angel' comes from the Greek word for 'messenger', *angelos*, so an angel is someone who is sent on an errand by God. In some parts of the Bible, it is impossible to tell whether this messenger is what we would call an 'angel', or just a person who happens to be carrying a message from God. But either way, they are only deserving of the title 'angel' if they are acting on God's instructions. Incidents of angels acting independently are not widespread, though we will see one or two instances where angels behave strangely, and we will also look at fallen angels, who act in opposition to God.

In this book, I shall be focusing very largely on the angels of the Jewish and Christian scriptures, and the traditions of angelology that they have fed. The Appendix at the end of this book outlines the sequence of the main stories about angels in Scripture, for ease of reference. But I am certainly not trying to  argue that all encounters with angels that do not fit into this tradition are untrue or meaningless. On the contrary; I find descriptions of conversations and meetings with angels moving, intriguing and challenging. People who have met angels feel a different kind of connection with each other and with the universe beyond what we can see and control. But perhaps that is what the angels are trying to achieve. Everyone who has met an angel has been made to feel not only important in their own right, but also *connected*. The angel does not arrive simply out of care for that one individual – though that is part of it – but also to demonstrate a pattern of care and planning that might run through the whole world.

So my underlying questions are about what angels tell us of our own longings, and what messages they might bring us about our place in the world, our connections with each other and our relationship with God – if we really listened to them.

*Archangel
Michael, one
of few
angels
named in
the Bible.*

CHAPTER 1

Introducing the Bible's Angels

The hierarchy of creation

The Bible speaks of a universe in which humans and animals are not the only living beings. There is a certain degree of interaction between other kinds of life and human life. For one thing, all have their source in God. As far as the Bible is concerned, there is no other way in which anything can come into existence, except by the will of God. There are not multiple creators or power sources or life-givers in existence, only God. Angels are not divine beings, but neither are they human. As in old translations of Psalm 8, a common biblical way of describing the relative positions of angels and people is to say that God has made human beings 'a little lower than the angels'.

Later, the New Testament letter to the Hebrews goes on to make the extraordinary claim that God, who makes both human beings and angels, chooses to come and live as a human being, lower than the angels, in the person of Jesus Christ, whom Christians believe to be the Son of God, who 'sustains all things by his powerful word'. Angels only come into existence through Jesus Christ, Christian writers argue, and yet Jesus is willing to join us lower orders, beneath the angels, so as to help us.

While the Bible gives us occasional glimpses of the activities and priorities of the other kinds of beings God has made, its real interest is in us human beings. The Bible tells the story of God's interaction with human beings, and so, generally, we only see angels as they relate to us. Now and then, one of the great prophets is given a brief glimpse into a heavenly world where angels have a life of their own in relation to God, but the minute the angels see the prophet looking, their activity refocuses itself, at God's bidding. People see angels when God wants them to, and so when angels realize that people can see them, the angels know that they have a job to do. It is a salutary thought that the universe might be full of lives in which we human beings are entirely peripheral. But angels at least seem to know that, for some incomprehensible reason, God cares passionately about human beings. Angels might prefer to be composing glorious angelic music, but they are happy to stop and run down the road to carry a message from God to some rather smelly, dirty, earthbound and stupid human being. Angels are in the know about God's strange plan to become a human being himself, so they are not in danger of underrating these creatures, however low in the general hierarchy of things they seem to be.

Busy angels

Our imaginations tend to fail if we try to think what the lives of angels might be like when they are not busy bringing messages to us. Either we have a pious but rather dull picture of angels hovering in mid-air and singing Bach cantatas, or we imagine that their lives are really very much like ours, with the same kinds of concerns that we have. Or, possibly, we imagine angels sitting around, watching our world as though it is a particularly engrossing soap opera, because they have nothing as interesting in their own lives. While that suggests a lack of imagination about what angels might be up to when they are not busy in the human world, we might be forgiven for that, because angelic activity does seem to come in clusters, rather than being continuous and steady. There are long periods of Bible narrative and of subsequent history where angels are hardly mentioned at all, and then other periods when scarcely a day goes by without a sighting.

Angels are visible only when God wants them to be.

Angels are busiest on errands for God when there are momentous things afoot – which makes sense, when you stop to think about it.

So in the Bible, a concentration of angels can be a pointer that something very special is happening. There are lots of angels near the beginning of God's relationship with his people, and again at the end of the physical world as we know it. And there are angels all around the story of Jesus, but they are also very active in the early years of the Christian community. At times when human beings were having to adjust their perceptions of God, it seems that we needed a bit of help from angels.

In Genesis, which is the book of the Bible that tells about the creation of the world and about human beings' first encounters with the God of the Bible, angels are very busy at one of the pivotal moments. This moment is when

God calls a particular man, Abraham, and gives him the opportunity to get to know God well. The calling of Abraham is the focal point for Christians, Jews and Muslims, all of whom know it as a moment when we discover something decisive about ourselves and about God's commitment to us. Angels are particularly active in relation to Abraham's children, because through these children, other people, too, are to be given the chance to share in Abraham's relationship with God. We shall meet Abraham and his children again, later in this book.

Angels come to the aid of the people when they are tempted to give up believing in God. Although the people of Israel believe themselves to be God's own people, that does not always protect them or give them victory. When they are captives in a foreign land, and there is enormous pressure to conform and to deny God, the angels are there as a sign that God does still exist, even in a foreign land, and that his people's loyalty is still to him, as his loyalty is still to them. This is actually a very important insight in the ancient world, where gods tended to be local and tribal. Angels helped Israel to notice that their God was everywhere, and could be worshipped under all circumstances.

In the Christian story, the angels are particularly noticeable around the time of Jesus' birth. God is doing something so unlikely in choosing to be born as a human baby, that the people directly involved need all the help they can get to see that this is indeed what is going on. Not that the angels are absent for the rest of Jesus' earthly life, but they play a slightly different role for Jesus and for his followers, as we shall see.

The earliest Christians, too, were facing a credibility gap, and needed a bit of angelic comfort and help. They were given the task of telling everyone that although Jesus had been crucified and buried, he was actually still alive and, what's more, he was the complete revelation of the nature and purpose of God. Not unnaturally, not everyone believed them, and Christians faced some severe tests and persecutions, as they still do in some parts of the world. Angels helped to free them from prison on more than one occasion, and angels encouraged them to take their mission outside the boundaries of Judaism.

It is particularly interesting to see angels at work to build up the early Christian church, starting with its natural leader, Peter. He had been a follower of Jesus from the beginning of his public service. When Jesus was crucified, Peter was so frightened of being involved in his fate that he denied that he knew Jesus at all. After the resurrection, the living Jesus made a particular point of asking Peter to take responsibility for all the new believers. This Peter, who had let Jesus down so badly, became the leader of the new Christian church, and one of its boldest preachers. The angels made sure that his ministry was not hampered by Peter being kept in prison for too long.

On several occasions, angels persuade disciples into action. Both Peter and another disciple, Philip, are directly brought to preach to non-Jews through the work of angels. Philip is directed by an angel to go and hang about on a road through the wilderness until, lo and behold, an influential official from the Ethiopian court comes riding down the road, searching for God. And there is Philip, ready and waiting, thanks to the angel.

In Peter's case, it is his potential converts who see the angel, and are instructed to send for Peter. 'He will give you a message by which you and your entire household will be saved,' the angel tells these people. Peter needs all the confirmation he can get that this really is God's will. He needs to know, both for himself and for the other leaders of the earliest church, that God really does intend to invite non-Jews into the Christian community. It was a highly contentious issue in the new community's life, so a bit of back-up from an angel was a great help to Peter as he baptized the Roman centurion Cornelius and his family.

Angels are very active, too, in the final book of the Bible, called 'Revelation'. It is a visionary and mystical book, with its focus on a time of great conflict between the forces of good and the forces of evil. The ultimate fate of the world and of all human life is bound up with the outcome of this conflict. Angels mark out those who are the servants of God, so that it is clear who belong to God and must not be harmed. Angels blow the trumpets that unleash destruction upon the faithless earth. Angels directly and loudly proclaim God's message of salvation and of judgment. An angel seizes the devil, who is also described as a dragon or a serpent, ties him up and imprisons him. An angel shows the book's author the 'river of the water of life, bright as crystal, flowing from the throne of God'. Angels are everywhere, militant, terrible, fatal to God's enemies, but strong, joyful and reassuring to God's faithful followers.

So although there may be a regular level of angelic activity in many parts of the Bible, there is a strong suggestion that angels are particularly active at times when God is doing something new, something that might make people feel insecure or threatened. When God calls Abraham, when Jesus is born, when the first Christians start to preach – at all these times God is doing something that will change human understanding of what God is like. That is always a frightening thing. People get very attached to their concept of God, and like to know that they are doing what God wants them to do. The promise to Abraham is a shift in the religious perspective of the time. God promises to be Abraham's God, but not just in the way that any tribal god might be said to belong to one people. God calls Abraham to take responsibility for the way in which all people will come to know God. Abraham is to be a picture of what the relationship between God and people should be like.

In Jesus, God does something even more extraordinary. He comes to live and die as a human being. It ought not to be possible – part of the definition of being God is exactly that God is *not* human. But God is refusing to wait until people come to him. Instead, he is going out to meet them and bring them home to himself. The first Christians have to tell the world that this is what God is really like. So at the time of Abraham, of Jesus and of the first church, angels redouble their activity to help people to trust that these shifts really are the work of God.

Then, when the final conflict comes, the time of ultimate choice between God and evil, angels are everywhere, making it plain what God wants. As the distance between heaven and earth closes, as the life of the earth draws to an end, the angelic realm becomes clearer and clearer. They have been

God's messengers to human beings throughout the centuries, but when time ends, both humans and angels will be able to be in God's presence, so no more messages will be necessary.

If this is how angels operate in the Bible, perhaps it is how angels also operate today. Angels do not appear simply to comfort and encourage and warn, but to move us on, to help us to make some imaginative leap or overcome some mental hurdle that is preventing us from seeing what the world might be like and what our own role in it might be. Angelic activity is exciting, but definitely not for the faint-hearted.

Gabriel, the best known angel in the Bible.

CHAPTER 2

What do Angels Look Like?

When is an angel not an angel?

Surely everyone knows what angels look like? They are beautiful, slightly androgynous figures, and they have wings. All poems, hymns and pictures that describe angels know that, after all. But the interesting thing is that there are very few actual descriptions of angels in the Bible, and where we do have clues about what they look like, they do not necessarily lead to the traditional picture.

Unlike human beings, the physical form of angels seems to vary. Sometimes they are indistinguishable from people. For example, Abraham is visited by three mysterious men, who tell him that his wife, Sarah, will have a son, although she is well past normal childbearing age. The only reason for calling these men 'angels' is that they carry a message from God, with information about the future which they could not know through any other means. This child of Sarah's is to be the centre of the promises between God and Abraham, and so he is vital to the whole of the rest of the story that the Bible tells. But Sarah does not believe them. She hides behind the tent-flap and laughs at this improbable message, which she would not be very likely to do if the messengers were ten feet tall, radiantly bright and winged. Her behaviour rather suggests that these angels are entirely ordinary in everything except the message that they bring.

There is an old saying that we should beware in case we find we are 'entertaining angels unawares'. If angels may be mistaken for human beings, then it is obviously sensible to treat all human beings with circumspection. The poet William Blake warns us to 'cherish pity, lest you drive an angel from your door'.

Other angels are instantly recognizable as such, even before they open their mouths. Dazzling light is one of the things associated with some angelic manifestations. The writers Matthew, Mark and Luke, who tell stories about the earthly life of Jesus, all describe the angels who wait for the disciples by the empty tomb of the risen Jesus as strikingly bright. 'His appearance was like lightning, and his clothing white as snow.' (Matthew)

There are other things, too, about angels that suggest that

their physicality is not exactly like ours. They can appear and disappear, for example, and are not uniformly visible. On at least one occasion in the Old Testament, an angel is seen by a donkey but not by the donkey's master. There is a strong suggestion that Balaam, the owner of the donkey, cannot see the angel because he is trying to avoid hearing what God is asking of him. He does not want the message, so he cannot see the messenger.

All of this might help to explain why there are few good descriptions in the Bible of what angels look like. Perhaps the categories with which we would normally describe physical beings do not really work for angels. The androgynous winged angel that is the standard representation in most fine art does not appear in early Christian art for several centuries. When the earliest Christian artists are painting the angel Gabriel telling Mary that she is to be the mother of Jesus, Gabriel is a human figure, and is only recognized as an angel by his clothes and by his context. When you know the story, it is obvious who he must be. But it looks as though early Christian artists are deliberately not using the conventions they would have found in non-Christian art for depicting divine messengers. It is not really until well into the fourth century that Christians feel confident enough that their story will not be misunderstood to use earlier conventions. After the Emperor Constantine became a Christian in the fourth century, Christianity spread so widely and became so well

known that it began to be able to define other traditions, rather than being defined by them. Angels and heavenly beings and other-worldly creatures exist in all religious traditions, but early Christian artists are trying to make a point about the way in which angels work in the Christian story. They cannot simply be assumed to operate like these beings from other settings. These angels obey the Christian God.

That is not to say that there is no biblical basis for our standard picture of an angel. We have already seen that angels can pass as human beings, and there are several places where they are described as having wings. For example, when the prophet Isaiah has the vision of heaven that gives him his prophetic commission, he describes the angelic beings he sees like this:

> In the year that King Uzziah died, I saw the Lord sitting on a throne, high and lofty; and the hem of his robe filled the temple. Seraphs were in attendance above him; each had six wings: with two they covered their faces, and with two they covered their feet, and with two they flew.
>
> **Isaiah 6:1–2**

The prophet Ezekiel, too, is directly given his task in a visit to the heavenly court. The beings he describes are very strange indeed:

> ... they were of human form. Each had four faces, and each of them had four wings. Their legs were straight, and the soles of their feet were like the sole of a calf's foot; and they sparkled like burnished bronze. Under their wings on their four sides they had human hands. And the four had their faces and their wings thus: their wings touched one another; each of them moved straight ahead, without turning as they moved. As for the appearance of their faces: the four had the face of a human being, the face of a lion on the right side, the face of an ox on the left side, and the face of an eagle; such were their faces. Their wings were spread out above; each creature had two wings, each of which touched the wing of another, while two covered their bodies. Each moved straight ahead; wherever the spirit would go, they went, without turning as they went. In the middle of the living creatures there was something that looked like burning coals of fire, like torches moving to and fro among the living creatures; the fire was bright, and lightning issued from the fire. The living creatures darted to and fro, like a flash of lightning.

Ezekiel 1:5–14

Each of these 'living creatures' is also accompanied by a strange, shining wheel within a wheel, covered with eyes, which moves when the creature moves.

Clearly, Ezekiel has a very strong, physical recollection of what he saw, but equally clearly, he is struggling to find the right language to describe it. Many artists have tried to draw creatures that have all the characteristics that Ezekiel lists, and found it surprisingly difficult. Ezekiel has only human words to describe something very definitely not human, as though he is seeing what no other human being has ever seen, which is the angelic beings in their natural habitat, not adapted for our human eyes.

The last book of the Bible, Revelation, also has several descriptions of angels at work. One of them is very like Ezekiel's picture, rather simplified, though with six wings rather than the four that Ezekiel sees:

> Around the throne, and on each side of the throne, are
> four living creatures, full of eyes in front and behind:
> the first living creature like a lion, the second living
> creature like an ox, the third living creature with a
> face like a human face, and the fourth living creature
> like a flying eagle. And the four living creatures, each
> of them with six wings, are full of eyes all around and
> inside.
>
> **Revelation 4:6–8**

Neither Ezekiel nor the book of Revelation actually calls these 'living creatures' angels, so perhaps they are something else entirely. Their main purpose seems to be to worship God, rather than to carry messages for him. Perhaps they are not among those beings whose regular duties involve interaction with people. But they do seem to be one of the main biblical sources, along with cherubim and seraphim, of the belief that angelic beings have wings, and wings persist in most images of angels, even if the other characteristics of these strange beings do not.

Angels with names and angels without

One possible way of explaining these differences in the way angelic beings are described is to assume that within the general category of what we call 'angels' there are several different types, so that to call them all 'angels' may be of as little descriptive use as calling human beings and cats 'mammals'. They have a lot in common, but that does not make them similar to look at.

Very few angels are named individually in the Bible. Gabriel is, of course. He plays a vital messenger role in announcing the coming birth of Jesus, but that is not his first appearance. He is also employed to bring a message to the prophet Daniel: 'while I was speaking in prayer,' Daniel says, 'the man Gabriel, whom I had seen before in a vision, came to me in swift flight at the time of the evening sacrifice.'

Gabriel is clearly one of those angels who can pass for human when necessary, though no one ever seems to question the truth of his messages, so there must be something very authoritative about him. Similarly, in the apocryphal book of Tobit, the angel Raphael accompanies young Tobias on his dangerous journey, without anyone knowing he is an angel until towards the end of the story. He has to tell them, 'I am Raphael, one of the seven angels who stand ready and enter before the glory of the Lord', before they realize. And very shaken they are when they find out that the person they have been treating more or less as a servant is actually such an exalted being.

The archangel Michael is also named. He is much more than a messenger – he is a warrior angel, and he fights against evil. In the book of Revelation, it says 'And war broke out in heaven; Michael and his angels fought against the dragon. The dragon and his angels fought back, but they were defeated.' So it seems that Michael is not a messenger in the ordinary sense, but one reserved only for occasions of the utmost seriousness, when God's purpose can only be achieved through battle. He does carry God's message, but it is a message that no words can make heard. His title 'archangel' tells us that he is in command of other angels, and that he is fearsome.

Tobias and his angelic travelling companion, Raphael.

Cherubim

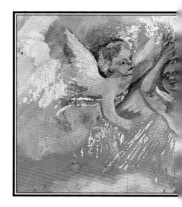

Other angels are not named as individuals but as types. So, for example, cherubim are generally classified as angelic beings. The cherubim of the Bible are not the plump, draughtily-clad little beings of classical paintings, but terrifyingly powerful beings. In the Bible's creation story, Adam and Eve disobey God and are forced to leave the peaceful garden where they had been made. The cherubim are placed at the entrance to the garden of happiness, the Garden of Eden, to ensure that no one can get back in. They stand with a flaming, turning sword, doing God's bidding without question, unlike the wretched human beings, who can only gaze back with longing.

No description is given of the cherubim, but they do seem to be associated with judgment. God rides on the cherub when he comes to defend his people. 'Smoke went up from his nostrils, and devouring fire from his mouth; glowing coals flamed forth from him. He bowed the heavens, and came down; thick darkness was under his feet. He rode on a cherub, and flew' (2 Samuel). This would be a frightening sight even to those whom God was defending, let alone to his enemies.

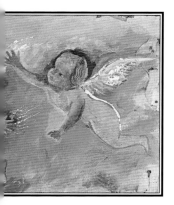

Cherubim protect the ark of the covenant too. The ark was a sacred and powerful container, which the Israelites took everywhere with them, until it found a permanent home in the Temple. It contained the blocks of stone which God had given to Moses, inscribed with the Law which represents the binding agreement between God and his people. Although the people of Israel were still nomads at this point, nothing about the construction of the ark is dictated by convenience. It is built of dark, heavy wood, and embellished with gold. The cherubim are made out of beaten gold, and their golden wings meet over the box, protecting it with their magnificence.

The ark with its watchful cherubim is a constant reminder to the people of what God requires of them. Israel's enemies quickly realized its psychological importance to the people, and tried to capture it in battle. If they succeeded, they soon regretted it. On one occasion, when the ark was seized by the Philistines and put in their own temple, it wreaked such havoc that they could hardly wait to get rid of it. It hacked the statue of their god (Dagon) to pieces in the night, so that it was found, headless and limbless, as though cut through with a sword. It caused plagues and death on such a scale that the whole city was decimated, and at this point the few remaining citizens quickly put it on a cart and took it back to the Israelites.

What emerges is a picture of the cherubim that associates them with fearful and merciless strength. It is used only in defence of God, but it is used without any of God's gentler characteristics, like compassion. The cherubim are an impartial force of judgment, and utterly terrifying as a result. Interestingly, they play no part in the story of Jesus. Is it fanciful to guess that beings like the cherubim might not entirely understand or approve of what God is doing in Jesus? Christian thinkers say that God comes to us in Jesus to open up a pathway home for us. Adam and Eve were forced to leave the Garden of Eden because of their sinfulness, but God does not give up on human beings. Instead, he comes to live with us in the form of Jesus, and offers to be close to us again. He offers to forgive us freely and make it possible for us to be at home with God, with each other and with the world again. If cherubim are associated with judgment, perhaps they do not understand this willingness on God's part to offer forgiveness without punishment. Cherubim might prefer to wield the flaming sword, if forgiveness is not part of their nature.

*Sword-wielding cherubim keep Adam and Eve
from returning to Eden.*

Seraphim

The seventeenth-century poet Milton speaks of the cherubim and the seraphim united in their praise of God. He pictures them vividly and, as so often with Milton's poetry, we can almost hear the music that he is trying to capture with his words. Milton nearly always describes God and his angels in the context of music. Where God is, there is singing and playing associated, as though Milton simply assumes that God and music belong together. He writes of a vision of heaven, where the 'bright Seraphim' stand in a 'burning row', playing their trumpets, while the cherubim sing and play their harps. So much is conveyed by Milton's images. Order is there. The cherubim and seraphim stand together like an orchestra, and play in harmony, working together to achieve their ends. But they are also unbearably bright – fire imagery and gold are necessary to convey this. We see an unimaginably brilliant and melodious court scene in Milton's mind.

Milton knows that the cherubim and seraphim are both like and unlike. Like the cherubim, seraphs are winged beings. They appear far less often in the Bible, where their main role is as God's attendants. With their six wings, they fly around the throne of God, exulting in their favoured position, and singing God's praises continually. But they, too, can be called angels, because they do interact with human

God receives continual praise from the seraphim.

beings at God's command. The prophet Isaiah is given his commission to speak God's words to his people by a seraph. The seraph takes a coal that has been burning incense on the altar in front of God, flies to Isaiah and touches his mouth with it, to purify this mortal being enough to receive God's message. If Isaiah feels any pain, he does not mention it, so overwhelmed is he by what is happening to him.

What we have to conclude, then, is that there are varieties of angels. Some are like human beings, and some are not at all. Some have wings, some do not. Some are dazzlingly bright, some are not. Some can be mistaken for people, and some definitely cannot. Some have regular duties with regard to human beings, some only occasional interaction, and some, perhaps, none at all.

These biblical angels have been rather domesticated and tamed by artists who, gradually as time went on, looked less and less at the descriptions in the Bible, and more and more at previous artistic conventions of depicting divine messengers. Perhaps it might be a good discipline, when we long for angelic protection, to imagine ourselves confronted with the many-headed creature with its eye-filled wheel. If an angel is not a nice chap with lovely soft wings and a white robe, but an elemental force of shocking power, we might realize that angels are not at our beck and call, but only at God's.

CHAPTER 3

Bringers of Good News

The acceptable face of angels

It must be fun to be one of the angels who brings good news. Although the main job of angels is to be God's messengers, whatever the message, it surely must be better to be allowed to be a messenger of good news rather than bad.

But that is not to say that angelic messengers of good news are necessarily received with champagne and cheering crowds. Clearly, some human beings are so shocked by the appearance of any angel that they are quite unable to distinguish between the proper treatment of a messenger bringing good news and of a messenger bringing bad. The messenger himself is so terrifying that it is hard to hear the message at all.

Angels can never have been far from Mary and infant Jesus.

'Do not be afraid'

A lot of the appearances of angels in the Bible have to start with the angels saying 'Do not be afraid', which must be frustrating for them, when they must be longing to deliver the message. For example, at the time of the birth of Jesus, angels visit a group of shepherds sitting in a field, and clearly terrify the wits out of the poor men. This seems to be partly because of a light phenomenon that is regularly associated with angels. In Luke's Gospel, we are told that when the angel appeared in front of the shepherds, he was surrounded by 'the glory of the Lord'. It is not entirely clear what this would have looked like, but it was probably very bright. This happened in an age before electric or neon light, when most people's eyes would only be used to firelight, candlelight and oil lamps. 'The glory of the Lord' was obviously in a different league. The shepherds' eyes were so preoccupied with the dazzle that it took them a while to hear words as well.

Presumably, first-century shepherds were, on the whole, ignorant and illiterate men who might be excused for not knowing all about angels. But in the Christmas story, an angel also visits someone who surely ought to recognize an angel when he sees one. Zechariah was a very respectable and religious man. He came from a long line of priests, and must have grown up with stories of angels. Yet one day, when it was his turn to be doing his priestly duty, offering incense in the sanctuary of the Lord, he is suddenly confronted by an angel, and is just as terrified as the shepherds. In his case, there does not even seem to be an obvious reason for terror. The shepherds were surrounded by 'the glory of the Lord', but Zechariah just looks up to see 'an angel of the Lord, standing at the right side of the altar of incense' (Luke). Presumably he had thought he was alone in the sanctuary of the Temple, so it must have made him jump at least when he looks up and sees the angel, but we are told 'When Zechariah saw him, he was terrified; and fear overwhelmed him.' (Luke)

To make matters worse, this devout man questions the angel. The angel has come to tell him that although he and his wife are technically a little on the elderly side for child production, they are going to have a baby. There are plenty of stories in the religious tradition in which Zechariah grew up about angels bringing news of the conception of a special child. But still Zechariah does not make the connection.

In reply to Zechariah's questioning, the angel says, 'I am Gabriel. I stand in the presence of God, and I have been sent to speak to you and to bring you this good news.'

The anger in Gabriel's voice is very obvious. He is important enough to stand in God's presence, where most people bow or kneel. He has agreed to bring this news because it is so significant and so joyful, and he does not expect some old man to question him. Zechariah's punishment for his stupidity is that he is struck dumb until

Angels
announce the
good news to
the shepherds.

the child whose existence he doubted is born.

His child is to be John the Baptist, whose job it is to tell the world who Jesus is. John is an integral part of God's great plan to save the human race. No wonder Gabriel was willing to bring the news, and no wonder he is so cross to be faced with such disbelief.

It does make you wonder if sometimes religious belief is a hindrance to insight. The shepherds certainly acquit themselves better than Zechariah. They are just as scared, but they do not question, and they follow their instructions without any hesitation. It is almost as though Zechariah has decided that his dealings with God and his angels are safely confined to the religious rituals he performs so assiduously. He does not expect them to break out into real life.

News of the resurrection

The angels who announce that Jesus, who was crucified and died and was buried, is alive again also meet with a very mixed reception. Again, they might have expected to be greeted with joy, but perhaps they have not realized how incredible is the message that they bring.

All of the four writers who tell the story of Jesus in the Bible agree that angels were involved in bringing the news of Jesus' resurrection out of the tomb and back to life. The earliest of the Gospels is the Gospel of Mark, and it is the starkest. The women who are the first people to visit Jesus' tomb find a young man, dressed in very white robes, sitting where the body should be. He tells them that Jesus is not dead any more, but they are so frightened that they just run away. Matthew, another early witness to the story of Jesus, agrees that the angel was very bright to look at. Matthew does not stick to Mark's rather unimaginative 'very white', but uses lightning and snow as ways of making us see just how bright this angel was. Luke agrees that the angel was 'dazzling', and both Matthew and Luke take the story up from where Mark leaves it. The women are dreadfully frightened, and they do not know whether or not to believe the angel, which is hardly surprising, since it is telling them that the man they saw dead and buried is now alive again. But that does not stop them from talking, and others begin to investigate their strange tale.

The fourth Gospel writer, John, concentrates on the story of one of the women who goes to the tomb. Her name is Mary Magdalene. All kinds of stories are told about her and it is hard to disentangle fact from fiction. But at the very least, Jesus had given her life new meaning and direction, and she was recognized as one of Jesus' best friends and followers. After his death, she is distraught and her grief focuses on an almost obsessive determination to find his mangled body and prepare it properly for death. Instead, when she arrives at the tomb, she meets an angel.

The encounter is almost comic because Mary does not really care who it is that she has met. For all we know the angel was twenty feet tall with lightning issuing from every feather of his magnificent wings. All Mary knows is that he is not Jesus and that Jesus' dead body is no longer there. 'What have they done with the body of Jesus?' is all she wants to know. She is not awed or frightened or thrilled or reassured, because she hardly notices his existence.

Do the angels sigh and cast up their eyes? Here they are, bringing the best and most exciting news the world has ever known, even better than the birth of Jesus, and no one knows how to react at all.

Or perhaps the angels are the best possible illustration of the old saying that 'virtue is its own reward'. Perhaps it is enough for them to have the pleasure of telling the news, however it is received. After all, they know God well, and they know they can trust him to make sure that eventually the value of what they have announced will be seen.

Saving Isaac's life

The angels know, as people do not, that life is God's business. They have had the pleasure before of intervening at God's command to save a life. Perhaps the most poignant occasion was when they had to save the life of Abraham's son, Isaac.

This is a story that Zechariah, the father of John the Baptist, should have known well, since it is one of the most important stories in the Jewish scriptures. Isaac is born after angels visit the elderly Abraham and Sarah, and tell them that, against all odds, they are going to have a child, and that this child will be the means by which God will raise a people to worship him and witness to him in the world. So a lot hangs on this child's life. The promise God makes to Abraham depends completely on the survival of this precious child.

But suddenly, God asks Abraham to sacrifice the child. He is to take his longed-for son up a mountain and kill him and burn his body as a sacrifice to God.

Unquestioningly, Abraham does as he is told. He and his son set off into the mountains, carrying fire and a knife. The boy begins to get a bit worried. He cannot help noticing that they have everything with them but the main course. Where is the animal to sacrifice? 'God will provide,' says Abraham grimly. But he has to go so far as to tie his son up and lay him on the pile of wood, ready to burn, before the angel arrives:

> When they came to the place that God had shown him, Abraham built an altar there and laid the wood in order. He bound his son Isaac, and laid him on the altar, on top of the wood. Then Abraham reached out his hand and took the knife to kill his son. But the angel of the Lord called to him from heaven, and said, 'Do not lay your hand on the boy or do anything to him; for now I know that you fear God, since you have not withheld your son, your only son, from me.' And Abraham looked up and saw a ram, caught in a thicket by its horns. Abraham went and took the ram and offered it up as a burnt offering instead of his son. So Abraham called that place 'The Lord will provide'.
>
> **Genesis 22:9–14**

'You don't have to do it,' the angel says. 'God does not require it.'

It seems that Abraham needed to know how far he really trusted God. Although his whole relationship with God, and everything that God had promised him, depended upon the boy Isaac, Abraham had to be prepared to give him up and still go on trusting in God. When he realized that nothing at all could shake his faith in God and his promises, then God gave it all back to him:

Angels in heaven celebrate the resurrection of Jesus.

Because you have done this, and have not withheld
your son, your only son, I will indeed bless you, and I
will make your offspring as numerous as the stars of
heaven and as the sand that is on the seashore... and
by your offspring shall all the nations of the earth gain
blessing for themselves, because you have obeyed my
voice.

Genesis 22:16–18

The angel arrived in the nick of time, and Isaac's life was
spared. Abraham and God are now closer than ever.

Quite what Isaac thought of it, we are not told. We have to
hope that he saw the angel and knew that God had sent his
messenger specially to save the boy's life. That might make
him like and trust angels more, but I doubt if he ever again
wanted to go for a long walk with his father!

But the angels who sit by the empty tomb of Jesus, who
should have been dead but was alive again, are telling a much
bigger story than that of Isaac and Abraham, vital as it is. The
story of Isaac and Abraham is a story of how God chooses to
teach a whole race about himself. He calls them and moulds
them so that they can tell the world what God is like.

The angels who announce that Jesus is to be born as a
baby on earth tell the world, Christians believe, that God is
sending his Son to live in the world, and to be God's loving
presence in this world that God has made. When Jesus grows

up and is put to death on the cross, the angels return three days after his death to tell everyone that death could not hold on to Jesus. So these angels come, according to the Christian story, to tell the world that Jesus is still alive and always will be; they are saying that even death cannot separate us from the love of God. God loves us so much that Jesus, God the Son, enters into our life and death, so that there is no part of our human experience in which we have to be separate from God. Wherever we are, even in suffering and death, God is there. The angels come to tell us this good news. The life of God runs through everything, even those things that look like death. Life is the nature of God, angels say, burning with the brightness of God's unquenchable vitality.

'He dreamed that there was a ladder set up on the earth, the top of it reaching to heaven; and the angels of God were ascending and descending on it.' (Genesis)

CHAPTER 4

Strange or Frightening Encounters with Angels

Jacob's angels

There are a number of very puzzling stories of encounters with angels in the Bible. At least two are associated with Jacob. Jacob is Abraham's grandson, and so the son of Isaac, whose own birth was announced by angels, and whose life was saved by an angel. But although Jacob is therefore aristocracy as far as the Bible story is concerned, that does not make him in every way a morally admirable character. On the contrary, he tricks his brother, Esau, in order to get the family inheritance from their old, blind father. But Jacob, for all his moral ambivalence, seems to have a sixth sense for the numinous and sees angels quite regularly. On one occasion, he is sleeping out of doors with a stone for his pillow and, not surprisingly, his sleep is restless and full of dreams.

'He dreamed that there was a ladder set up on the earth, the top of it reaching to heaven; and the angels of God were ascending and descending on it' (Genesis). Jacob takes enormous comfort from this dream. He understands it to mean that, despite his perfidy, God has not abandoned him. But it is a very strange dream. Why should the angels need a ladder? They have wings, and other means of appearing and disappearing. Perhaps Jacob's dream suggests that there are certain places where it is easier to access angels, just as there seem to be certain people who are more receptive to them.

But perhaps that is not accurate. Perhaps it is more that certain people and places – or cultures – have lost their ability to see angels, whether by deliberately blocking them, or by not using the necessary skills enough. We are used to the idea that those in 'primitive' cultures, who are more directly dependent upon nature for their survival than we are, can still follow animal traces across tracts of land where we can see nothing, or can predict the weather by watching the sea and sky. We who have more or less constructed our own environment do not need those skills any more. We have technology to do it for us. That particular closeness of connection with nature has atrophied in us, on the whole. Perhaps our angel antennae have likewise withered away. We think we do not believe in angels or need them any more, so we do not attend to the signs.

Jacob found his dream of the ladder between heaven and earth consoling. For him, it meant that whatever he had done to cut himself off from God, God and the angels would find their own ways of reaching him. That angel ladder is not to be found only in Jacob's dream, or in a wilderness thousands of miles away and thousands of years ago. It is a dream that can be shared by anyone, anywhere, who is prepared to feel Jacob's hope. Jacob's ladder, where the angels go up and down, is not some distant place, but can be found wherever we are prepared to acknowledge our need. It is not that the angels have withdrawn from us, but we from them. Turn back again, say the angels, as they climb up and down the ladder.

Equally odd is the story of Jacob wrestling with the angel. Once again, Jacob is on his own, at night, outside. He has prospered since cheating his brother, Esau, but now the time has come for the two brothers to meet again. Jacob has sent all of his party on ahead to the meeting place, with presents for Esau, hoping to placate his brother before he has to meet him. He stays by himself one more night before facing up to the consequences of what he has done.

> Jacob was left alone; and a man wrestled with him until daybreak. When the man saw that he did not prevail against Jacob, he struck him on the hip socket; and Jacob's hip was put out of joint as he wrestled with him. Then he said, 'Let me go, for the day is breaking.' But Jacob said, 'I will not let you go, unless you bless me.' So he said to him, 'What is your name?' And he said, 'Jacob.' Then the man said, 'You shall no longer be called Jacob, but Israel, for you have striven with God and with humans, and have prevailed.'
>
> **Genesis 32:24–28**

This is another of those occasions when angels are not immediately distinguishable from human beings, but Jacob is in no doubt of the significance of what has happened. He knows that he has met God's messenger, and has paid a price for the past and been given a new future, symbolized by his new name.

This story has inspired artists, poets, psychologists and philosophers down the ages. It encapsulates so much about the necessity of facing what we have done, the cost of our selfishness, and the ability to move on to a new future that does not deny the past but is not wholly conditioned by it. The angel inflicts real pain on Jacob because that is what Jacob knows he deserves. He cannot accept his new name until his hip socket is put out. The angel's action is both punishment and forgiveness; both a warning and a sign of hope.

Christian writers, like Charles Wesley, have taken this angel to be a symbol of Christ. In one of Wesley's hymns, he talks to the 'Traveller Unknown', and the hymn is so personal that it sounds as though Wesley is speaking out of his own experience. He describes Jacob's determination to go on wrestling with the stranger until he finds what he is looking for. Wesley seems to see this as a metaphor for the religious search. We will not find answers if we are not prepared to struggle for them. Wesley, like Jacob, believed that he had found his answer. He believed that he had found out the name of the unknown person he wrestled with, and that name was 'God', or 'Love'. Like Jacob, he believed that the price he paid for this knowledge was worth it. Jacob was left with a limp, and Wesley says that he too is content to limp for the rest of his life, because his limp reminds him that he cannot walk in his own strength. Wesley believes that it is only in admitting his weakness and dependency, his 'halt' thigh, that he can learn to rely on his real strength, which is God's love. But to know your weaknesses and use them as strengths is good advice for Christians and non-Christians alike.

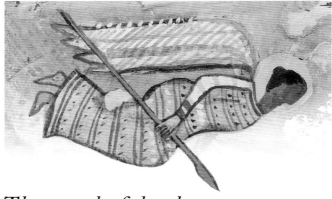

The angel of death

Jacob's angels are not the only ones who suggest that angels cannot be taken lightly. They can be fierce as well as comforting, as Lot and his family could testify.

Lot lives in a place called Sodom, a place whose name has become synonymous with a particular kind of offence against God. Two angels arrive to warn Lot and his family that Sodom is about to be destroyed. The angels are treated to the typical behaviour of the town's inhabitants, who want to rape them. Attempting to rape an angel is not a sensible plan. The angels are more than capable of defending themselves. But although they save Lot, because God has told them to, they do not bother too much with details. Some of Lot's family get left behind in the town, and Lot's wife looks back on her home and is turned into a pillar of salt. Where once there was a thriving city, there is now only heat and smoke. The angels were told to wreak destruction, and they have done it with great thoroughness.

A similarly horrifying story is the one about the angel of death who attacks an army that had come to fight against God's people. The Assyrians seemed indestructible, but an angel kills them all in the night. To call him the angel of death seems highly appropriate, since the storyteller says that one hundred and eighty-five thousand soldiers died in one night. The king of the Assyrians escapes temporarily, but he too is killed, by his own sons. The angel of death is nothing if not thorough.

These are hard stories to interpret. They raise questions about the nature of God, if angels really are just messengers, carrying out orders. It is tempting to believe that the angels exceeded their orders, and that the writers of the Bible assumed that they were obeying God because the end result worked in favour of God's people.

There is certainly a story where Abraham is directly in conversation with God without any angel intermediaries, and Abraham appears to persuade God not to destroy a city full of people.

> Then Abraham came near and said, 'Will you indeed sweep away the righteous with the wicked? Suppose there are fifty righteous within the city: will you then

sweep away the place and not forgive it for the fifty
righteous who are in it? Far be it from you to do
such a thing, to slay the righteous with the wicked,
so that the righteous fare as the wicked! Far be that
from you! Shall not the Judge of all the earth do
what is just?'

Genesis 18:23–25

In the Bible, this extraordinary conversation between God
and Abraham follows very quickly after the story of the
angels who visit Abraham and his wife Sarah and tell them
they are going to have a special child, through whom God
will bless all the nations of the earth. And at once it is as
though Abraham feels a sense of responsibility for his people.
The angels have made him a promise, but Abraham knows
instinctively that angels' promises cannot be applied selfishly.
The promise is not just to him, Abraham, who so desperately
wants a child, but also, through his child, to all those others
whose hearts long to believe in God and to trust in God's
promises for the world. So now, as Abraham bargains for the
lives of the people in Sodom, he is learning to be a leader of
his people. He is learning to feel responsibility and
compassion for others. He is learning not to want to use God
simply for his own selfish means. Does this conversation
really change God, or is it Abraham who is changed by the
end of it?

It is intriguing to speculate that this might be one of the things that God loves about people. People question and change and learn. People's hearts can be moved and enlarged. People can love each other unselfishly, with compassion for and joy in the other person, for their own sake, not for anything they bring to the one loving. In other words, people can learn to be a little bit like God. The nature of angels seems to be rather different. Angels seem to be very black and white beings, living with absolute certainties rather than nuances. If they think God does not like something, they destroy it, without waiting to see if it could learn or change.

Hearing angels

In the sense of black and white behaviour, angels and animals have more in common than angels and people. There is a wonderfully comic story in the Bible of an occasion when an angel communicates better with a donkey than he does with the donkey's master. The donkey's master is a prophet called Balaam. King Balak has sent for Balaam to come and curse the king's enemies, and Balaam is in a terrible quandary. On the one hand, he would very much like to do the king a favour, because doing favours for kings is generally profitable. But, on the other hand, Balaam really is a prophet. He can only say what God tells him to say, and God tells him that he is not going to curse the king's enemies, but bless them. So Balaam dithers, not knowing whether or not to go with the king's messengers.

In the end, he sets off, hoping against hope that God will change his mind and allow Balaam to do what the king wants. But as the prophet rides along on his donkey, an angel with a sword bars his path. Balaam is so busy trying to manipulate God that he does not see the angel. But the donkey does.

> The donkey saw the angel of the Lord standing in the road, with a drawn sword in his hand; so the donkey turned off the road, and went into the field; and Balaam struck the donkey, to turn it back on to the road. Then the angel of the Lord stood in a narrow path between the vineyards, with a wall on either side. When the donkey saw the angel of the Lord, it scraped against the wall, and scraped Balaam's foot against the wall; so he struck it again. Then the angel of the Lord went ahead, and stood in a narrow place, where there was no way to turn either to the right or to the left. When the donkey saw the angel of the Lord, it lay down under Balaam; and Balaam's anger

was kindled, and he struck the donkey with his staff.
Then the Lord opened the mouth of the donkey, and
it said to Balaam, 'What have I done to you, that you
have struck me these three times?... Am I not your
donkey, which you have ridden all your life to this
day? Have I been in the habit of treating you in this
way?'... Then the Lord opened the eyes of Balaam,
and he saw the angel of the Lord standing in the road,
with his drawn sword in his hand.

Numbers 22:23–31

The donkey and the angel, though so different, share an
obedience and a certainty about what they are for. The
donkey knows it was bred to serve Balaam, the angel knows
it exists to serve God, and both simply get on with what they
are made for. But although Balaam knows that he is born to
be a prophet of the Lord, that does not make matters simple
for him in the way that it apparently does for the donkey and
the angel. Human beings always seem to introduce an
element of choice and uncertainty into everything we do,
even though we generally know, in our heart of hearts, what
the right thing is. We make our own lives harder, to say
nothing of those of donkeys and angels. But perhaps that is
part of our nature.

'Warning angels' do not always face quite so many
obstacles in delivering their messages. Paul was one of the

earliest Christian missionaries, who spent a lot of his life travelling round the Europe of his day, preaching the Christian message. He himself had been suddenly converted to Christianity, and he spent the rest of his life trying to get other people to believe what he had come to believe. Travelling was never straightforward in the first century, and Paul faced all kinds of hazards on his travels. On one occasion, he was caught up in a terrible storm at sea, when an angel came to tell him that he and all the people on the ship would live. Paul's work was not yet finished. Over and over again, Paul reassured his shipmates, and his calm certainty spread to them, even though they had seen no angel. Paul said to them:

> 'I urge you now to keep up your courage, for there
> will be no loss of life among you, but only of the ship.
> For last night there stood by me an angel of the God
> to whom I belong and whom I worship, and he said,
> "Do not be afraid, Paul... God has granted safety to
> all those who are sailing with you." '
>
> Acts 27:22–24

This angel did not need a sword to make himself understood, and Paul seems to have been able to hear him quite clearly. It is not obvious from the way Paul tells his story whether he actually saw the angel, or just felt his presence, standing

Joseph receives an angelic warning in a dream.

close. Either way, he is in no doubt about what has happened.

Joseph, too, hears and believes an angel's warning. Joseph is the man who is to be like a father to Jesus. He is to marry Mary and help to bring up the baby Jesus. The angel comes to Joseph in a dream, and tells him to take Mary and the baby Jesus far away, quickly, because they are in danger. Even though the message comes in a dream, which might easily be dismissed, Joseph does not doubt what he has heard and he instantly takes his family out of harm's way. It is interesting that the angel should find it easier to speak and be heeded in a dream. Perhaps people are more open to hearing when their minds, rational in the daytime, are in the dream world.

The angel has been sent to Joseph because the wicked King Herod is plotting to kill all boy-children under a certain age. He has heard of the existence of Jesus and is afraid that Jesus will be a challenge to his own power and, since he does not know exactly where Jesus is, he hatches this ruthless plot. We long for the angel to warn all the other families about what Herod is going to do. But the angel is sent only to Joseph. As Joseph, Mary and Jesus live quietly in Egypt, their home town is full of the sound of weeping mothers, mourning over their butchered sons.

Why did God not send his angels to save all the innocent children, either then or now? That is one of the great unanswerable questions. Although you could argue that it is not God's fault but Herod's that the children died, as it is so often the fault of human beings, now and throughout history, still the ultimate responsibility is God's. If he exists, he made the world with these possibilities. He made people capable of love, but also of hatred, capable of generosity, but also of monstrous selfishness. Was he right to take such risks in making us? That is the ultimate question that religious and irreligious people alike must face. For some, it is the reason for disbelief. For everyone, it remains an aching question. Perhaps the best interim response to it is a passionate commitment to making sure that we try to reduce the number of Herods born into the world. If we could really see how much human evil we could wipe out, we might be in a better position to see the world as God created it. Then perhaps the angels would not have to bring so many warning messages.

CHAPTER **5**

Guardian Angels

An angel of our own

Several of the hymns that are sung by monks and nuns as part of their night-prayers invoke angels. It is very understandable that we should want angelic protection at bedtime, when we feel most vulnerable and unable to defend ourselves, and are particularly glad to think that our never-sleeping angel might be standing beside us all night.

When people think of angels at all, they probably think of guardian angels. In English, the term has become so common that someone who escapes accident by sheer luck is often said to have a 'guardian angel'.

Guardian angels are the acceptable face of angels. We would rather not wrestle with the problems caused by

*The role of
angels is
sometimes
to offer
protection.*

thinking about the angel of death. But the thought of a supernatural person whose whole job is to see that we come to no harm is much more acceptable. It is just what all of us would like, for ourselves and the people that we love.

What's more, the traditions of guardian angels are deeply embedded in Christian thinking throughout the centuries. Elgar's great musical work, *The Dream of Gerontius*, is based on a poem by John Henry Newman about someone being brought by their angel to meet God at the throne of judgment. It perfectly represents the tradition that each of us is given into the keeping of a guardian angel, from our birth to the moment of our death.

There are a great many people who testify to the existence of such angels. Many, many people are sure that they have been saved from road accidents or other kinds of fatal errors by the direct intervention of an angel, and these angels are testified to throughout the centuries. In the past, the majority of people who met an angel were religious believers, but encounters with angels do not seem to have diminished in our increasingly secularized Western world.

The Bible does not seem to have a concept of a guardian angel in that particular way. Instead, the much more normal role of angels in the Bible can involve them being protectors of human beings for a particular purpose and for a set period, but not for life.

On a number of occasions, angels feed people, generally when they are in the wilderness, with no food or water around, and in real danger of death. For example, God sends an angel to Hagar and her son when they have been turned out to die by Sarah because of her jealousy. Sarah is Abraham's wife, and she has just, most unexpectedly, given birth to a boy when she had given up all hope of ever having a child. She knows her son is important to God, but she gets madly protective of him, and begins to hate Hagar and her son. Hagar was Abraham and Sarah's servant and had already given Abraham a son called Ishmael. This was a situation that Sarah seemed to tolerate before the birth of her own precious child, but afterwards she is consumed with jealousy, and forces

Hagar and the child out into the unforgiving desert.

Hagar is in despair after days of wandering:

> When the water in the skin was gone, she cast the child under one of the bushes. Then she went and sat down opposite him a good way off, about the distance of a bowshot; for she said, 'Do not let me look on the death of the child.'... and the angel of God called to Hagar from heaven, and said to her, 'What troubles you, Hagar? Do not be afraid; for God has heard the voice of the boy where he is. Come, lift up the boy and

hold him fast with your hand…' Then God opened
her eyes, and she saw a well of water. She went, and
filled the skin with water, and gave the boy a drink.

Genesis 21:15–19

It is such a poignant story. Although Sarah's son Isaac is the
heart of God's promises to Abraham, God is not a jealous
mother. He sends an angel to bring Hagar hope, and she
finds water. She and her son flourish in the desert where they
were sent, knowing that even if Abraham and Sarah have
thrown them out, God has not.

An angel also comes to take care of the prophet Elijah in
the desert. Elijah has got into terrible trouble and his life is in
danger because he has faithfully proclaimed the word of God.
Unfortunately, the word of God happened to be an outright
condemnation of King Ahab and his wife, Queen Jezebel,
who are now out for Elijah's blood. Elijah is tired, frightened
and fed up. He obviously feels that there are serious
drawbacks to being God's prophet, and he would quite like to
stop. If the only way to stop carrying God's awkward
prophecies is to die, he would rather die of hunger and thirst
in the desert than of torture in the king's dungeons.

But God sends an angel to feed Elijah.

[Elijah] went a day's journey into the wilderness, and
came and sat down under a solitary broom tree. He

asked that he might die. 'It is enough: now, O Lord, take away my life…' Then he lay down under the broom tree and fell asleep. Suddenly an angel touched him and said to him, 'Get up and eat.' He looked, and there at his head

was a cake baked on hot stones, and a jar of water. He ate and drank, and lay down again. The angel of the Lord came a second time, touched him, and said, 'Get up and eat, otherwise the journey will be too much for you.' He got up, and ate and drank; then he went in the strength of that food for forty days and forty nights.

1 Kings 19:4–8

It was obviously no ordinary food, if it could sustain the prophet like that. But it is a particularly nice touch that the angel brought warm cake rather than dry bread. The angel is preparing Elijah not just for a long journey, but also for an encounter with God. At the end of his forty-day journey, Elijah is sitting on God's holy mountain, waiting. He ignores a strong wind, an earthquake and a fire, but when he hears silence, he goes out to meet his God. The God who sends an angel to feed his old servant is not interested in terrifying him. He speaks with intimacy, and promises Elijah that very soon he will be

Angels

*Angels keep
Daniel safe in
the lions' den.*

able to pass his irksome job on to someone else.

Angels are also prepared to act as waiters for Jesus in the
wilderness. As soon as the adult Jesus realizes what God is

asking him to do, he goes out into the desert to test his vocation. We are told that he is tempted by Satan, who tries to make Jesus use his power for his own ends. For forty days, Jesus resists, and when he is triumphant, the angels cluster around, taking care of him.

Angels also guard Daniel when he is thrown into a den of lions. Daniel is a faithful Jew who is working for a non-Jewish monarch, King Darius. Daniel is a very able young man, and soon advances to a position of considerable authority, much to the annoyance of many of the king's other officials. They decide to trap Daniel by persuading the king to issue an edict saying that no one is to worship anybody but the king. They know that Daniel will not be able to obey this edict, and sure enough, he is soon discovered worshipping God. Much as Darius would like to exempt him from the law, he knows that his own authority is on the line, so Daniel is thrown into the lions' den.

But in the morning, there he is, unharmed, because an angel came and made the lions keep their mouths shut all night. Daniel is saved, and King Darius gains considerable respect for Daniel's God. 'He is the living God, enduring for ever. His kingdom shall never be destroyed, and his dominion has no end. He delivers and rescues, he works signs and wonders in heaven and on earth; for he has saved

Daniel from the power of the lions' (Daniel).

These angels who feed Hagar, Elijah and Jesus, and protect Daniel and others, are in one sense guardian angels. But their guardianship is temporary. They do a particular job for a certain length of time, whether it be baking warm cakes or holding lions' mouths shut. But when the job is done, off they go again.

Sometimes the task is longer. For example, when God leads the people of Israel out of captivity in Egypt, under the leadership of Moses, they are accompanied by an angel, and by a pillar of cloud by day and a pillar of fire by night. Whether these pillars are actually angels, or just the work of angels, is not clear, but they both guide and protect. They show the people which way to go, and they keep the people's position hidden from the pursuing armies of the Egyptians. These angels may have been employed for several days, or even weeks, but their task too comes to an end.

Angels of the churches

There do appear to be angels who live with people forever, but the people are not individuals but communities. In Revelation, John writes to the seven churches of Asia about the messages he has been given for them in visions. Each of the messages is addressed to the angel of that church. So, for example, the angel of the church at Ephesus is commended for patient endurance, but warned that its early love of God has cooled.

Revelation is a mysterious book, full of the activity of angels, both good and bad. It is hard to be sure exactly what these 'angels of the churches' are, but whatever their original function, they have taken on the characteristics of the community that they represent. They have lived through much with their communities, and have become so identified with them that God's message can simply be addressed to this angel, as though to the whole community. If they are 'guardian' angels, then they are not wholly successful. They are not preserving their communities from error or saving them from persecution. It is possible that they are not strictly 'angels' at all, but the leaders of the churches. But if so, perhaps they are called 'angels' because they should have been guarding their communities, and they need to be reminded to do so more vigorously, now that the final conflict between good and evil is approaching.

But if there is not a fully-developed notion of the guardian angel in the Bible, there are at least two highly suggestive avenues of thought about what the function of such beings would be, in God's eyes. First, the angel brings God closer to human beings. 'For he [God] will command his angels concerning you to guard you in all your ways' (Psalms). The guardian angel is the personification of God's care for each person. Sometimes God can seem very distant and impersonal, and at such a time, the angel, so much more like us, can help us to feel God's care again.

Secondly, guardian angels also remind us that if we are precious to God, so are other people. In Matthew's Gospel, Jesus warns, 'Take care that you do not despise one of these little ones; for, I tell you, in heaven their angels continually see the face of my Father in heaven.' This odd verse comes in the middle of several sayings of Jesus that make it clear how much he values children. There is only one step, he warns, between children and God – the child's angel. Anything done to a child will instantly be seen by their angel and so by God.

This, then, is the religious heart of the notion of guardian angels. They remind us of how much God loves and cares for each one of us individually. God's love is not just a huge, impersonal force, but directly shaped to the needs and characteristics of each of us. This concern, this angel, is with us from the moment of our birth until we meet God face to face, after our death. But the same is true of others too. God does not have favourites. He loves each person with the same kind of personalized love. Our guardian angels are not at liberty to sacrifice others to get the best for us, because everyone is surrounded by the same care.

The belief in guardian angels is very widespread in the Christian tradition, from early times. But this is what angels do. They are not there necessarily to keep us safe or to get the best deals in life for us. They are there to bring us to God, whatever that may take. It may be superficially comforting to think that we have an angel with us at all times, but if the role of that angel is dictated not by what we think would be best for us but by what the angel decides, it might be rather less attractive. What if our angel does not consider that it has to keep us safe and happy at all times? What if it sees its role as more like a heavenly personal trainer, urging us, spiritually speaking, to eat sensibly and take more exercise? The path to heaven might not always be the most comfortable path, but it is the one that the guardian angel is there to keep us on.

Guardian angels, in this way of thinking, are there

constantly to remind us of God's love and God's priorities. If we listen to them, this tradition suggests, we will know how much we mean to God, and we will know how God loves every other person we interact with. Our angels will bring out the best in us by drawing us more and more towards God's way of caring for each other. If we invoke our guardian angels, we should expect them to be true to their nature, and to make us more and more attuned to God's people and God's world.

We might prefer the notion of an angel who is entirely on our side, as utterly biased as a doting parent who refuses to see any wrong in their child. We long for a being who loves us like that, but has a lot more power. But instead, angels might be offering us the love of God, who sees us just as we are, with all our faults, and still loves us unconditionally. Out of that never-ending love, our guardian angels will look with patience on our selfishness and stupidity, and will keep on helping us to find the best in ourselves, the compassion, love, trust and hope that are most like God. If we will let them, if we will really pay attention to them, perhaps our guardian angels will guard us against our worst selves, and help us to be what God intends us to be.

CHAPTER **6**

Fallen Angels

The nature of angels

Angels are not God. Like everything else that exists, the Bible says, angels come into being out of the overflowing vitality of God. That means that, unlike God, they are not perfect. They can choose, as human beings do, whether to live with God as their primary focus, or with themselves as their primary focus. The Bible assumes that angels are closer to God. Whatever their physical nature is, it is not as different from God's as human nature is. So the angels can live in the heavenly place with God in a way that human beings cannot.

Human vocabulary fails in its attempts to describe where the 'heavenly place' is. Since we are not capable of thinking of a 'place' that has no boundaries of space or time, our imaginations always locate heaven 'somewhere'. The prophets who have had a glimpse of God and the angels struggle to find words to convey what they 'saw'. The prophet

Rebellious
angels are cast
out from
heaven.

Isaiah talks about the Lord 'sitting on a throne, high and lofty; and the hem of his robe filled the temple'. Already there is a paradoxical description – is God 'in' the temple? Or is he so vast that his hem engulfs the whole temple? It is very doubtful if the prophet could have answered such a question, but he is sure that God is surrounded by angelic beings.

Another prophet, Daniel, agrees with that, and says that God shares his 'place' with uncountable numbers of angelic beings; 'ten thousand times ten thousand,' Daniel says, trying to convey the vastness of what he has seen in his vision.

It is tempting to presume that God and his angelic company do not occupy a different 'place', in physical terms, from ours, but simply that they do not occupy physical space at all. Occasionally, individuals may get a glimpse of a bigger world co-existing with ours, and sometimes angels take a shape that is easier for our eyes to see and our imaginations to grasp.

The Christian scriptures believe that Jesus Christ is the 'image of the invisible God'. He is the means by which anything outside God has any understanding or vision of God at all. He is the bridge that God provides between himself and the different worlds that he has created, and so he is also the bridge whereby angels become visible to us. Jesus says that people will see 'the angels of God ascending and descending' upon him. He is the new Jacob's ladder. He is, the Bible seems to imply, the way in which angels are able to reach out to us, just as he is the way in which we are able to know God.

So the angels are created beings, as we are, and they come to their knowledge of God through the means that God himself provides, as we do, rather than through their own closeness to him. Angels may look limitless, powerful and magical to us, but compared with God, they are very small and ineffectual. That means that, like us, angels are capable of getting things wrong. They are capable of confusing good and evil, and they are capable of getting things out of perspective, and putting themselves in God's place. According to the Jewish scriptures, this is the big temptation of human beings, to long to be what only God can be, and it seems that the temptation is the same for all created beings, even angels. Some angels manage to resist, but some do not.

The Jewish and Christian scriptures are not hugely interested in fallen angels, at least not in the way in which later literature is. Their motivation is not explored, and nor are the ultimate questions about how evil comes to exist in a universe created by a good God. The Bible simply notes the existence of evil, and knows that it is not concentrated only in human beings. Instead human beings are caught up in a struggle that affects all realms of creation, seen and unseen, between God and creatures who try to be God. The Bible is also utterly convinced that there is only one possible outcome to this struggle, because only God is God. But for those who are still in the middle of it, the triumph of God's goodness is not always so evident.

Lucifer

There is only one fallen angel who has a name in the Bible, and that is Lucifer. Even that may be a description of what his role was – the Day Star – rather than an actual name. He is generally also assumed to be properly identified as Satan. The prophet Isaiah describes Lucifer's rebellion against God like this:

> How you are fallen from heaven, O Day Star, son of Dawn! How you are cut down to the ground, you who laid the nations low! You said in your heart, 'I will ascend to heaven; I will raise my throne above the stars of God; I will sit on the mount of assembly on the heights of Zaphon; I will ascend to the tops of the clouds, I will make myself like the Most High.' But you are brought down to Sheol, to the depths of the Pit.
>
> **Isaiah 14:12–15**

Already two key elements of the continuing story of Lucifer or Satan are present here. The first is that it is pride and envy of God that motivates Lucifer, and the second is that his defeat is certain. He is condemned to inhabit the regions of the dead and so, by implication, has lost his own immortality.

If Satan longs to be God, that would explain why he assumes that others do too. The snake who tempts Adam and Eve in the Garden of Eden is often identified with Satan, partly because that is exactly the inducement that is offered to the two first human beings to make them disobey God. The snake tempts them to eat the forbidden fruit by telling them that it will make them like God. Sure enough, they fall for it, because they too long to be more powerful, just as Lucifer does.

All through the Bible, the foreground story is about the relationship between God and people. But every so often, in the background we see another struggle going on, involving angels and other kinds of beings. There is outright war between God's angels and Satan and his angels, apparently. The archangel Michael is particularly identified as God's warrior angel, who is involved in regular pitched battles with Satan, right up to the end of the physical world. 'War in heaven!', the biblical news headline writers shriek.

Paul, the Christian missionary leader of the first century, also talks of 'principalities and powers'. These have sometimes been identified as types of angels, but they seem to

*Archangel
Michael, God's
heavenly
warrior.*

be playing a game of their own. They are neither wholly bad, like Satan and his angels, nor wholly good, like Michael and his. Instead, they are a kind of independent order, who can impinge on human beings. They are among the things, Paul says, that used to be able to confuse us and separate us from God, before the coming of Christ. It is not, apparently, that they are interested in ultimate confrontation with God, as Satan is. They are simply neutral, concerned only with themselves. But the trouble is that, against the background of the cosmic struggle between good and evil, neutrality is not really possible. The 'principalities and powers' are like looters in a war. They can destabilize the situation drastically, while not being interested at all in the outcome of the war.

In this universe full of strange creatures, human beings easily get confused, it seems. We have enough sensitivity to spiritual beings to suspect that they exist and even, occasionally, to encounter them, but we are not always very good at working out what kind of attention and respect they deserve. Human beings much too easily assume that other less physical beings are powerful and should be respected or propitiated, rather than referred to God. Paul gives his converts a very simple rule of thumb for dealing with angels. If they tell the good news of Jesus Christ, they are trustworthy; if they do not, then you can safely ignore them. However these beings might choose to describe themselves, if they are not singing from this hymn sheet, then they are among the powers that Jesus Christ frees us from, as far as Paul is concerned.

Jesus himself says that he saw the moment when Satan fell from heaven 'like a flash of lightning' (Luke). This is generally assumed to be describing the same incident as Isaiah speaks about. But Jesus tells his friends about this to explain why they are now free from the power of Satan and can help to free others. His followers are discovering that when they use Jesus' name, they can cure people and

free them from the kinds of diseases associated with evil.

Very early on in his adult ministry, Jesus and Satan come face to face, and Satan tries to tempt Jesus with the urge to power that he found worked so well with Adam and Eve. But in this case, he fails. He tries to make Jesus use power for self-protection and self-aggrandizement, but Jesus will not. Jesus will only use his power in obedience to God. From now on, where Jesus is, only God has power, and that protection is extended to all who use Jesus' name.

As so often in the Bible, we see a world that is like multiple transparencies imposed upon each other, so that we get blurred views of all of them. On the one hand, in life we genuinely experience conflict between good and evil, in which we and our whole world are involved, with the fear, pain and death that this entails. On the other hand, the Bible assures us that the outcome of this conflict is already known. God is the victor. No other result is possible in the world that God makes. The New Testament argues that the only place where these two realities coincide is in Jesus Christ. Jesus lives in the world of conflict and death and separation from God, but is always obedient only to God. He never for one moment acknowledges the possibility that anything or anyone but God will triumph. That means that even when the forces that reject God bring Jesus to the horrible death on the cross, that death itself becomes, through Jesus' commitment to God, a place where God is still triumphant. So where people stand under the protection of Jesus, goodness has won, even in fear, pain and death. These things no longer have any hold, because the life of Jesus, which is the life of God's victory, has triumphed in all the situations where the fallen angels once held power.

We have to go on living with both of those realities – the reality of the fallen angels, and the reality of God's victory. The temptation is to try to take on Michael the archangel's role, and fight the battles ourselves. But we are not angels, and the danger is that we will begin to get interested in our own importance and the role that we are playing in this great drama. The safest thing to do, if we take Paul's advice, is to leave the angels to fight the angels, while we invoke God's victory through Jesus Christ and try to use it to free each other.

Chapter 7

Angels and Jesus

Announcing the birth of Jesus

If angels have busy times, then the time of Jesus' birth is one of the busiest. In Jesus, the Bible says, God is doing something so unexpected that human beings are going to need a lot of help if they are to believe that this is true. God is going to send his Son, Jesus, to be born as a baby. God the creator is going to come to live as part of his creation. No wonder the angels have to polish up their wings and get flying.

The archangel Gabriel seems to have been the leader of project 'Get God born'. It is Gabriel who visits Mary, to tell her that she is about to become Jesus' mother. This is obviously one of those occasions when Gabriel really looks

Gabriel tells Mary she will give birth to the Son of God.

like an angel. Although he is not described, Mary is in no doubt about what she is seeing. But she does not really understand the message.

> But she was much perplexed by his words and
> pondered what sort of greeting this might be. The
> angel said to her, 'Do not be afraid, Mary, for you have
> found favour with God. And now, you will conceive in
> your womb and bear a son, and you will name him
> Jesus. He will be great, and will be called the Son of
> the Most High, and the Lord God will give to him the
> throne of his ancestor David. He will reign over the
> house of Jacob for ever, and of his kingdom there will
> be no end.' Mary said to the angel, 'How can this be,
> since I am a virgin?' The angel said to her, 'The Holy
> Spirit will come upon you, and the power of the Most
> High will overshadow you; therefore the child to be
> born will be holy; he will be called Son of God…'
> Then Mary said, 'Here am I, the servant of the Lord;
> let it be with me according to your word.' Then the
> angel departed from her.
>
> **Luke 1:29–38**

There is something very touching about this conversation between Mary and Gabriel. Gabriel is gentle and patient with this human girl. He knows how important this whole thing

is to God, and he does not want to frighten Mary off. He answers her questions as fully as he can, and he tries hard to find the words that will help her to understand just how vital this baby is going to be. And Mary catches the vision and says 'yes'. She could have said 'no', but Gabriel has done his work well, and God has chosen Mary carefully.

The angels have to spend a lot of time reassuring people in this period before Jesus is born. It must have been quite a hard balancing act for the angels. On the one hand, they needed to appear in all their majesty so that people could really see that they were angels and take their message seriously. But on the other hand, they did not want to frighten people so badly that they ran away or passed out. Most of the Christmas angels have to start their messages by saying 'Do not be afraid', just as Gabriel does to Mary.

Some months later, when Jesus is born, the angels are again saying 'Do not panic' – to a group of shepherds, this time.

Then an angel of the Lord stood before them, and the glory of the Lord shone around them, and they were terrified. But the angel said to them, 'Do not be afraid,

for see – I am bringing you good news of great joy for
all the people: to you is born this day in the city of
David a Saviour, who is the Messiah, the Lord. This
will be a sign for you: you will find a child wrapped in
bands of cloth and lying in a manger.' And suddenly
there was with the angel a multitude of the heavenly
host, praising God and saying, 'Glory to God in the
highest heaven, and on earth peace among those
whom he favours!'

Luke 2:9–14

What a privilege for these shepherds. They not only see one
angel, who has a message just for them, but they
also see the joyful excitement of the flock of singing
angels. They must have told the story of that night
for years to come. What a good thing they were
several of them – one shepherd on his own would
certainly never have been believed. These angels,
too, have judged well, because as soon as the angels
vanish, the shepherds set off to find the baby. They
do not ask any of the sensible questions, like 'Why
would God send hosts of his angels to tell a bunch
of shepherds what he is doing?'. They tingle with
the excitement of the angelic singing, and run to do
as they are told.

What comes across is how excited the angels are

at what God is doing. They are thrilled to be involved in God's plan, and fly across the world, singing out the good news. Perhaps angels, who live between God and human beings, feel the separation between humanity and God most bitterly. Perhaps they long for the time when human beings can communicate with God as freely as they can, and they do not keep having to say 'Do not be afraid' whenever they talk to them. The angels understand that God is working to bring the human world and the angelic world back together, and they are excited to be a part of it. They understand that Jesus is going to be God's way of living in the world of human beings, and so of making a permanent connection again between human beings and God. Angels have very long memories, so perhaps they can think back to the time, at the dawn of creation, when God and human beings were as close as God and the angels are still. When the Bible imagines this time, it pictures a garden in which God and his first human beings, Adam and Eve, walk and talk together freely. So now, with the birth of Jesus, perhaps the angels think that earth will be like that garden again. God will walk in it, through Jesus, and talk to people again.

But, sadly, it is not going to be that simple. The part the angels play in the birth of Jesus is as messengers of joy, but then they have to sit back and watch the whole thing apparently going horribly wrong. Because although Jesus walks and talks with people, they do not all believe that he is speaking for God. They do not all respond to him with love and longing. Jesus has to suffer and die, and God will not let the angels intervene, much as they long to.

There are lots of pictures of the events around the birth of Jesus. Some of the world's greatest painters have imagined what it was like, and many of them include the angels in what they depict. But the angels seem less pervasive in the pictures of the rest of Jesus' life and death on earth. And yet they are there, watching and waiting, hoping for the word from God that would allow them to go and interfere.

Angelic restraint

At some of the hardest moments for Jesus we can almost sense the agonizing impatience of the angels. They are on tenterhooks. Quite early on in Jesus' ministry, he has to go out into the desert and face temptation. Before he starts preaching and teaching in public about God, and healing and performing miracles in God's name, he has to go away alone and put himself to the test. He has to be sure that he can do all of this for God alone, without any desire for fame and glory for himself.

In the desert, the devil, the fallen angel, tries to get Jesus on his side. He tries to make Jesus choose power for himself, rather than directing attention to God. The devil tries to make him turn stones into bread; he offers him all the kingdoms of the world if Jesus will worship him, instead of God. He takes him up a high tower and asks him to test God's love for him by throwing himself off the top. After all, the devil says, 'He will command his angels concerning you, to protect you,' and 'On their hands they will bear you up so that you will not dash your foot against a stone' (Luke).

Jesus resists the devil's temptations and then, at last, the angels are allowed to come to his aid. They cannot come to him before he has chosen, they cannot help him to make his choice, but once he has chosen God and refused the devil 'the angels waited on him' (Mark).

There is at least one other time in Jesus' life when we can practically see the angels hopping from foot to foot as they try to restrain themselves from dashing in too soon. It comes towards the end of Jesus' life, when his enemies are closing in on him. He knows that quite soon he will have to face a horrible death, and he prays for the courage to bear it. 'Then an angel from heaven appeared to him and gave him strength,' the Bible says (Luke). The angel does not rescue Jesus, nor does it stand in its shining glory and frighten his attackers into believing in Jesus. It simply comes to him, when no one can see, and gives him strength by its companionship. How much more the angel longed to do, we can only guess.

As Jesus goes on praying that night, out in the open and with just a few of his followers with him, Judas, who had been a

Jesus resists the temptations of fallen angel Satan.

friend of his but had turned against him, leads a group of soldiers to arrest him.

> Judas, one of the twelve, arrived; with him was a large crowd with swords and clubs... Suddenly, one of those with Jesus put his hand on his sword, drew it, and struck the slave of the high priest, cutting off his ear. Then Jesus said to him, 'Put your sword back into its place; for all who take the sword will perish by the sword. Do you think that I cannot appeal to my Father, and he will at once send me more than twelve legions of angels?'
>
> **Matthew 26:47–53**

The angels are dancing about, begging Jesus to ask for their help, but he does not do so. He knows they are there. He can sense their presence, and almost feel the comforting strength of the angel who had been with him just a few minutes ago. But he will not ask them to do what they long to do. Just imagine the effect that twelve legions of angels, with

Angels longing to rescue Jesus from the cross.

wings and blindingly bright armour, would have had on the pitiful rabble who have come to lead Jesus away to his death. But Jesus will not let them show themselves.

Angels do not die, so they watch with horror as Jesus shares the fate of all human beings and goes to his death. This is a part of God's plan that even the angels cannot make comprehensible. Perhaps they do not understand it themselves. The poet and hymn-writer of the eighteenth century, Charles Wesley, writes about this idea in one of his hymns. He says that the mystery of what God is doing in allowing Jesus to die on the cross is something that even 'the first-born seraph' tries in vain to understand. Angels who have been sent in the past, so they believe, to destroy whole cities and armies who dared to oppose God's people are now not permitted even to frighten those who kill God's own Son, Jesus.

As the angels watch Jesus on the cross, perhaps they remember the joy with which they announced the birth of the baby Jesus, and weep as they see what he has come to, as he hangs on the cross and dies in agony. But they do not interfere. Even now, at this moment of horror, they obey God. They trust that God knows what he is doing, and that the death of Jesus on the cross must be a terrible necessity. God plans to bring the human world and the divine world back into contact with each other, even if that means that Jesus must die. No part of the human world will be separated from God, not even death. The death of Jesus is to mean that even death is full of the presence of God.

If we imagine the life and death of Jesus as a series of pictures, or tableaux, we can play a kind of 'hunt the angels' game as we look through the pictures. In the first ones, where we see the pregnant Mary, or the newly-born Jesus, there are plenty of angels, and we can easily spot them. But as the story goes on, the angels are banished to the edges of the pictures, and their faces become sadder and more worried. They wring their hands and gaze on Jesus. They are angels, and they are used to appearing in different physical shapes, so they are not confused by the human Jesus. They recognize in him the Son of God, the one with whom and through whom they and all creation have come into existence. They know that God is now recreating, making a connection again between God and the world, through Jesus. But they wish it did not have to be this way.

CHAPTER **8**

Angels after the Bible

The changing face of angels

Angels have exercised the imaginations of artists in every medium in most ages, so that it is hard to know where to begin in exploring some of the developments in our understanding of angels that have taken place after the writing of the Bible. Although personal stories of encounters with angels are in some ways the most powerful witnesses we have, they do not necessarily make it easier for us to see what angels are for, and what their continuing function might be. The writers discussed in this chapter all make contributions to the theory of angels.

Music is often seen as part of angels' heavenly worship.

Worshipping angels

People who believe in God see worship as the primary activity of angels. The Bible would uphold this idea. We have already seen that when human beings catch a glimpse of the angels (before the angels are aware of it), they see angels clustered round God, singing and praising their creator. Most of the Christmas hymns about angels pick up on this aspect, too, and imagine angels in full song, pausing only to give their message and then returning to the music.

If God is the source of everything and deserving of praise, it is perhaps good to know that some part of creation always recognizes how vital God is and celebrates that fact appropriately. Certainly, human worship is much more sporadic.

But the great seventeenth-century Anglican theologian, Richard Hooker, takes this idea rather deeper. It is not just that God's ego needs the constant massaging of the worship of the angels, but more that the whole universe that God has designed is based on affirmation. The Bible believes that God makes the world out of love, not because he has to, but just because he wants to. Love is the real meaning of the universe. But that true, deep meaning is so often concealed from those of us who have to live in the world. The way we treat each other makes it harder and harder for us to believe that we are lovable or capable of giving love to others.

Only God's angels, of all the created beings, never lose sight of the love of God. They live so close to God that they do not need reminding. They are able, effortlessly, to give back to God the love that is shown to them in their creation. But they are also able to mirror God's love back to us. They are slightly more accessible to us than God sometimes is, because, like us, they are created beings. This is how Hooker puts it in *The Laws of Ecclesiastical Polity*:

> Beholding the face of God, in admiration of so great
> excellency they all adore him; and being rapt with the
> love of his beauty, they cleave inseparably for ever
> unto him. Desire to resemble him in goodness maketh
> them unweariable and even insatiable in their longing
> to do by all means all manner of good unto all the
> creatures of God, but especially unto the children of
> men: in the countenance of whose nature, looking
> downward, they behold themselves beneath
> themselves; even as upward, in God, beneath whom
> themselves are, they see the character which is
> nowhere but in themselves and us resembled.

The angels can look both up and down and make connections for us. They can carry our praise of God when we are not praising, and they can remind us, through their messages, of God's love for us. They play a significant balancing role in the world.

Angels with psychology

But, of course, not all angels are content simply to spend their days in worship of God. Just as we can lose touch with God, so, apparently, can angels. The Bible is not very interested in why this is possible. It tells the story of Lucifer's disobedience to God as straightforwardly as it tells the story of Adam and Eve. Both Lucifer and the first human couple demonstrate what the Bible takes to be plainly true, which is that the things that God makes have the possibility of rejecting God. The Bible does not have one single theory about how a good God who makes a wonderful world can have built in the possibility of evil. Instead, it tends to concentrate on what God does about it, once that possibility is loose in creation. It tells the story of how God acts, over and over again, to restore relationships with human beings, culminating in the coming of Jesus who is, so the New Testament says, God himself, come to live with us.

But the question of how evil comes into existence has exercised the imaginations and consciences of all generations. For many people, this is the reason for atheism. A good God could not create such a world, therefore there is no God. Believers would want to argue that it is the high price paid for genuine human freedom of choice. There can be no real love that is not freely chosen, so if we are created unable to do anything but worship God, then we cannot genuinely love either God or each other.

Some of the most creative thinking about this troubling issue has come through imagining what might make us want to rebel against God. If God does exist and is our creator and does love us and yet not coerce us, whatever would make us choose to reject such a God? The seventeenth-century English poet, John Milton, famously explored this idea in his extended poem, *Paradise Lost*. At the heart of the poem is Lucifer, the bright angel, who turns against God.

Milton unravels Lucifer's motives with startling realism. Lucifer lives so close to God and with such understanding of God that he knows God's value. The problem is that it makes him jealous. He longs to be like God himself, because he sees that there can be nothing better in the whole world. It is this mixture of appreciation and envy that makes Lucifer such a powerful study of motivation. Lucifer would not envy God if he did not realize God's worth. So it is, in a sense, one of Lucifer's best qualities that leads to his downfall.

Lucifer acts on his jealousy, too, in a way that is illuminating. Instead of trying to be like God by modelling himself on God's goodness and kindness and creativity, he tries to be like God by grabbing what God has. He thinks that if others give praise and worship and obedience to him instead of to God, then he will be like God, forgetting that the reason why praise and worship are offered to God is because of what God is already like.

So Milton describes how Lucifer persuades other angels to join him in a war against God. Lucifer needed followers to boost his own self-image. If other angels did not join him, then how could he possibly convince himself that he was equal to God? But when he loses his battle, and he finds himself exiled from heaven, he tries to persuade himself that this is just what he always wanted. 'Better to reign in hell, than serve in heaven,' Lucifer tells himself (*Paradise Lost*, Book 1). How far Lucifer has come from his original ambitions. He wanted to be like God. Now he is content simply to be in charge of anything.

What Milton's great poem does is to give Lucifer a personality. Inevitably, that personality is based on an understanding of what drives us human beings. In Lucifer, we see our own faults magnified. We see our pride, our determination to be in control, our unwillingness to be a minor character when we want always to be centre stage, our readiness to manipulate other people in order to make them serve our ends, whether that is for their good or not. Milton is not really trying to describe what might actually have happened in heaven. Instead, he is trying to provoke us into examining our own motives. He wants us to see the extremes to which our selfishness can drive us, and the consequences they might have for the whole world.

In this, Milton may actually have something in common with the contemporary British novelist, Philip Pullman. Pullman and Milton come from entirely different theological premises, but they both use the idea of 'war in heaven' to stimulate people into seeing how our choices shape the world. But where Milton sees Lucifer's pride as the quintessence of sinfulness, Pullman sees it as the heroic human ambition to take responsibility for our own world. Pullman does not believe in God, and he sees Milton's psychological study as a way of describing the human struggle for adult freedom and responsibility. As far as he is concerned, there must be 'war in heaven' if we are to throw down the 'envious' God that Milton's Lucifer thinks he is battling.

Pullman's brilliant trilogy, *His Dark Materials*, repays reading on any showing, but for our purposes it is interesting in its depiction of the angels Baruch and Balthasar. Baruch and Balthasar come to help the two children, Will and Lyra, who are the heroes of Pullman's story. But we learn that, although they are both angels, they have different routes to angelic nature. Balthasar says, 'Baruch was a man. I was not. Now he is angelic.'

Here, Pullman articulates a long tradition that angels are

not necessarily a different order of creation from human beings. Some human beings may become angels. In colloquial imagery, we call any good people 'angels', and much literature and pious imagining assumes that those who are dead can watch over us, like angels. There is no strong biblical backing for such beliefs. Although the Bible does argue that people who live in relation to God live forever, that does not mean that they become angels at death. The Bible assumes that angels and people are different kinds of creatures, just as people and animals are.

Pullman's angels also have quite human feelings. Baruch and Balthasar are deeply attached to each other, so much so that when Baruch is killed, even in his angelic form, Balthasar mourns him deeply and inconsolably. This too is part of traditional thinking about people, angels and death. We cannot bear to think that the people we love may live on after death but without the kind of attachment to us that we understand and still feel for them. All kinds of human hopes and fears about death are present in our traditions of angelic life.

Pullman is not interested in expounding theology. He tells a compelling story with consummate skill, and his aim is to encourage us to build 'the republic of heaven', where there is no need of God or any other hierarchy, but where human beings work together for the common good. But because of his knowledge of literature, his myth of the war in heaven inevitably builds on the hopes and fears expressed in earlier literature that does profess belief in God.

Christian hope for life after death challenges the clinging longings that are expressed in these traditions. We do not need to believe that our loved ones become angels or that they have nothing better to do than go on obsessively concentrating on us with the kind of single-minded love that Baruch and Balthasar display in Pullman's book. Instead, the Bible argues that our belief in life after death is based on our understanding of the unquenchable life of God. It is God's love and God's life that we are searching for in all our lives and our loves here on earth, and when we are reunited with God after death, we will know that we can trust those we love absolutely to God. We do not need to hang on and take care of them ourselves. We can wait in love and trust until we are reunited with them in God.

Christian and non-Christian angels

Unlike Philip Pullman, C.S. Lewis is a consciously Christian writer who chooses to try to convey a picture of what angels might be like by using non-Christian categories. In his science fiction trilogy, Lewis re-imagines some of the Bible's story in terms of interplanetary aggression and alien intervention. His 'angels' are aliens, whom our human myths have cast as gods and heroes. In the final volume of the trilogy, *That Hideous Strength*, Lewis describes the effects of meeting these 'angel aliens'.

> The whole room was a tiny place, a mouse's hole, and it seemed to her to be tilted aslant – as though the insupportable mass and splendour of this formless hugeness, in approaching, had knocked it askew.

Lewis very deliberately avoids the descriptions of brightness and terror that the Bible uses to describe angels, but he tries to convey the same sense of some being that does not fit our categories. His phrase 'formless hugeness' is one that might ring bells with many who claim to have met angels.

Towards the end of the same book, Lewis's alien angels come again, and this time they are more clearly differentiated and have different effects on the human beings who meet them. One of the angels is described as:

> ... strong like a mountain: its age was no mere morass of time where imagination can sink in reverie, but a living, self-remembering duration which repelled lighter intelligences from its structure as granite flings back waves, itself unwithered and undecayed, but able to wither any who approached it unadvised.

There are many ways of portraying what angels might be like.

Another is very different:

> Before the other angels a man might sink; before this
> he might die, but if he lived at all he would laugh. If
> you had caught one breath of the air that came from
> him, you would have felt yourself taller than before.
> Though you were a cripple, your walk would have
> become stately; though a beggar, you would have
> worn your rags magnanimously. Kingship and power
> and festal pomp and courtesy shot from him as sparks
> fly from an anvil. The ringing of bells, the blowing of

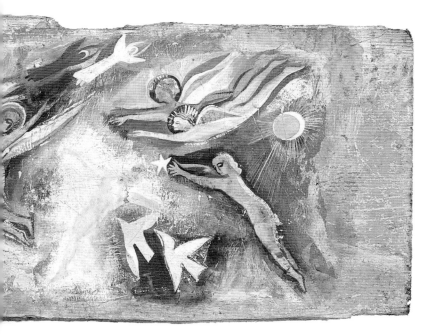

trumpets, the spreading out of banners are means
used on earth to make a faint symbol of his quality.

Our readings of the biblical descriptions of angels suggest,
just as Lewis does, that although all angels are terrifying,
some are terrifyingly joyful, while some are inhumanly
terrifying. Many of the narratives of encounters with angels
come from people who are not necessarily religious believers,
and Lewis is offering them other ways of describing what
they have met. As a Christian, Lewis does believe that, in the
end, these descriptions can be interpreted by the Bible's

understanding of angels, but he also opens the door to other truthful and sensitive ways of portraying angelic encounters.

Angels as wish-fulfilment

Yet, however many people say that they have met angels, the majority of people do not think that they have, and so many do not believe in angels. They see talk of angels as a way of avoiding talking about our real hopes and fears. Instead of facing our vulnerability, we talk about guardian angels; instead of taking responsibility for our own actions, we blame war in heaven for the state of our world; instead of acknowledging that we are the only rational beings in the universe, we try to make the empty void of space cosier with angelic beings who are both like and unlike us.

The existence of angels, like the existence of God, cannot be proved or disproved. It will remain a matter of faith, at least, until the end of the world. But although there are all kinds of reasons for doubting angels, and although some descriptions of meetings with angels are probably no more than consolatory fictions, perhaps we could argue that the proof of the pudding is in the eating.

For example, those who wish to cast doubt on the existence of angels might well point to the description given to us by Teresa of Avila of her encounter with an angel as a very typical piece of wish-fulfilment by a frustrated middle-aged nun. This is how she describes what happened to her in her *Life*:

> I saw an angel close by me, on my left side, in bodily
> form. This I am not accustomed to see, unless very
> rarely. Though I have visions of angels frequently, yet I
> see them only by intellectual vision... He was not
> large, but small of stature and most beautiful – his face
> burning as if he were one of the highest angels, who
> seem to be all of fire: they must be those whom we call
> Cherubim. Their names they never tell me; but I see
> very well that there is in heaven so great a difference
> between one angel and another, and between these
> and the others, that I cannot explain it.
>
> I saw in his hand a long spear of gold, and at the
> iron's point there seemed to be a little fire. He
> appeared to me to be thrusting it at times into my
> heart, and to pierce my very entrails; when he drew it
> out, he seemed to draw them out also, and to leave me
> all on fire with a great love of God. The pain was so
> great, that it made me moan; and yet so surpassing
> was the sweetness of this excessive pain, that I could
> not wish to be rid of it. The soul is satisfied now with
> nothing less than God.

Teresa of Avila lived in Spain in the seventeenth century.
Although she was a lively and attractive young woman,

interested in sex and marriage, she dedicated her life to God. The description she gives of this particular encounter with an angel is, to our post-Freudian ears, very obviously sexual, as the famous sculpture by Bernini makes clear. Yet the fact remains that Teresa drew great strength from this meeting, and that she was able to stand up to the Inquisition and to travel all over Spain, reforming the order of nuns to which she belonged. Those who wish to dismiss her angel story as middle-aged wish-fulfilment have also to find an explanation that deals with her obvious sanity and well-functioning life. She cannot easily be categorized as someone with delusional and pornographic visions. Whatever she experienced, or believed she experienced, gave her the strength and humanity to do what needed to be done.

Myriads of angels

Angels have appeared in so many stories, films, plays, adverts and pictures that my choice of literature to discuss may well appear idiosyncratic. Many people have their own favourite stories of angels, and if I have not written about them, I can only apologize. The examples I have chosen illustrate particular questions that, for me, angels can bring to the surface.

Milton helps us to explore why people might not believe in God. Pullman raises the question of human and non-human angels, and of emotions after death. Lewis enables us to think about how we might talk about angels if we do not think Christian categories make any sense, and Teresa of Avila makes us reassess angels and our own needs and longings. Angels are a way of talking about ourselves in our deepest need but also in our greatest strength, and that is something to which all angel-related literature bears witness.

Afterthoughts: Angels and God

We live in a big universe, whose possibilities we do not yet fully know or understand. While this is exciting, it is also frightening, as the unknown can often be. For many people, angels are the comforting face of this unknown universe. We do not entirely understand them, but we know that they are both like and unlike us, and that they are essentially benevolent towards us.

It would be nice simply to call a halt to our investigation of angels at this point. But if we do, we will miss most of the glory of angels. Angels are more complicated, more challenging, more exciting and more nuanced than this simplistic picture of a cosmic teddy bear.

The first thing that comes into sharp focus if we really concentrate on what is said about

angels in religious traditions and in the other encounters with angels that people describe is that angels are not just there to serve us. On the contrary, as far as angels are concerned, we are a small part of a much larger action that we can only occasionally glimpse. In biblical terms, we and the angels and the whole of the created universe are caught up in God's action to bring us back into relationship with himself. In mythical terms, we and the angels are part of the cosmic struggle between good and evil. The Bible does not see evil as a power in any way comparable to good, so it offers assurance that good will ultimately win, because God is good. But because God will not force our choices, but will only offer and encourage, we may not always, in our day to day life, feel the strength of God's goodness. We may often feel that evil is actually more powerful.

The angels, too, are part of the struggle to define what kind of a universe this is to be. Not all angels are on the side of the good, and this means that we human beings need a way of discerning whom to trust, whether we are talking about other human beings or other creatures in this baffling world. We need a context in which to put what we are offered. We need to be able to see how an angelic messenger fits into the overall moral picture of the world that we are building up in our daily lives and choices.

That instantly complicates our relationship with angels. We cannot treat them as always and invariably comforting. Sometimes, the comfort they offer us may be spurious. They may simply be encouraging selfish, self-protecting instincts in us. The angels who visited the shepherds at the time of Jesus' birth told the shepherds to leave their duty and go on a seemingly pointless errand to see a newborn baby. There was nothing in this message that brought the shepherds any obvious personal advantage. It did not make them safer. On the contrary, it risked getting them the sack, presumably, if they got back to the fields and found that a wolf had eaten the sheep in their absence. The shepherds could not know, when

they ran to see the baby, that they were writing themselves into a story that has been told for two thousand years now. They could not know that they would for ever afterwards be identified as the first people to recognize Jesus as God's Christmas present to the world. The shepherds obeyed the angels because they were unselfish enough to feel the joy of the angels and respond, whether that would do them any good or not.

It is not wrong to long for comfort, security and protection. It is entirely understandable that we should ache to bury our faces in the angels' heavenly feathers and never come out. But while people who have met angels do describe this sensation of being safely held, they also describe it as temporary. These moments of knowing ourselves to be safely held cannot continue forever. If they did, we would be like children who were never allowed to try anything or take any risks for fear of danger. Such children could not grow up, and neither could we.

So to set out on this voyage of discovery about angels is to commit ourselves to being connected into a bigger picture of the universe. We too become part of the story that God is telling about the world. A belief in angels commits us to a belief in a cosmos that is bigger than anything we can see or understand. And so it also commits us to playing our part in that cosmos. We cannot believe in angels and simply expect to be able to concentrate on our own needs and desires. These two ways of living in the world are mutually exclusive. We can either live in our own small world, where we need serve nobody but ourselves, or we can live in a world of angels, people, principalities and powers, which will commit us to action in helping to shape what kind of a world this will be.

If we choose to acknowledge the angels' world, we will not always be protected. But our lives will have a bigger meaning. Like the shepherds, we will be stepping into a story of the

way the world is going, and we may find that we too are spoken of for centuries to come, as part of the movement to recognize the world as belonging to God. The angels of the Bible are God's messengers. That is their job, their self-definition. We do not have to hear their message, and we can choose wilfully to ignore everything about them except the bits that we like for ourselves. But we cannot change their nature and function.

Behind, around, underneath and through the day-to-day world that we inhabit is the song of the angels. It is beautiful, endless, joyful and terrible. It will be sung whether we join in with it or not, but imagine the sensation of stepping into that angelic harmony and being caught up in its power and majesty. This is what the angels invite us to do. They long to teach us their song, so that we, with them, can sing a hymn of praise to the glorious universe and its maker.

Appendix: Angels in Scripture

Creation

God makes the world and the first people to live in it. But Adam and Eve disobey God, encouraged by the fallen angel who has already rebelled against God. Adam and Eve have to leave the Garden of Eden. The cherubim, with a flaming sword, prevent human beings from re-entering the Garden.

Abraham

God chooses Abraham to be the father of God's people. Angels come to tell Abraham and Sarah that they will have a child, and after the child is born, an angel prevents Abraham from sacrificing this son, Isaac. An angel also protects Ishmael, Abraham's illegitimate son.

Jacob

Jacob is one of Isaac's sons. He sees angels quite regularly, including angels going up and down a ladder between heaven and earth. Jacob also wrestles with an angel.

Moses

Several generations after Jacob, Moses is sent to rescue God's people from slavery in Egypt. They travel through the wilderness, looking for a land of their own, and are accompanied by an angel, and by a pillar of cloud by day and one of fire by night. God gives Moses the Ten Commandments – laws about how God's people are to behave. Moses and the people make the ark of the covenant to keep the stone tablets of the law in. The ark has golden cherubim carved on it. It is a holy and terrifying object, with the power to kill if it is taken away from God's people.

The People of Israel

After wandering in the wilderness for some years, the people of God find a land, which they take ownership of after a number of battles, and have to defend with force ever afterwards, sometimes gaining ground, sometimes losing ground. Sometimes the people of Israel are helped in battle by angels, who kill their enemies for them. Sometimes they are not. They are led first of all by judges, then by kings. Prophets also have a role in the kingdom of God, giving people words from God. Elijah is fed by an angel when he has to flee from the anger of King Ahab. Sometimes Israelites are taken prisoner, and have to live and work in other countries. Daniel is protected by angels when he works for a king who does not believe in God.

Jesus

By the time of Jesus, Israel has been conquered and occupied by the Romans. Angels announce the birth of Jesus, and stand around him as he lives on earth.

The Early Church

After Jesus, his followers are also protected by angels on a number of occasions.

The End of the World

Angels, led by the archangel Michael, take part in the final battle between good and evil. They will be involved in all aspects of the final end of the earth and the coming of God's direct rule.